Mini Mathematical Murder Mysteries

A Collection of Blackline Masters for ages 11-14
Jill Whieldon

Tarquin Group
www.tarquingroup.com

Publisher's Note

This was the first appearance of Jill Whieldon's Mini Mathematical Mysteries, followed by the volumes below. The price now includes electronic resources - which can be downloadable activities from Tarquin Select (www.tarquinselect.com) or printable versions of this title. For more details see www.tarquingroup.com/vouchers

You can keep up to date with this and other new titles, special offers and more, through registering on our website for our e-mail newsletter or following us on Twitter or Facebook.

Other Titles in the Series

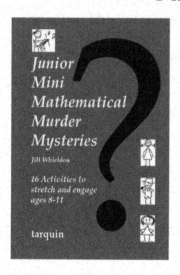

Junior Mini Mathematical Murder Mysteries ...for ages 8-11

and

More Mini Mathematical Murder Mysteries ...for ages 13-15

Published by Tarquin Publications
Suite 74, 17 Holywell Hill
St Albans
AL1 1DT   www.tarquingroup.com

Copyright © Jill Whieldon, 2011
ISBN: 978-1-907550-10-2

Distributed in the USA by IPG
www.ipgbook.com
www.amazon.com & major retailers

Distributed in Australia by OLM
www.lat-olm.com.au

Printed in the United States

Introduction

We all like to think we can solve a murder given the right clues. Here's a chance to use mathematics skills to identify "whodunnit".

The topics covered in this book are all included in the year 7 & 8 schemes of work in mathematics, so are aimed at the 11-13 age group. The tasks have been used successfully with older pupils too as a reminder of topics covered previously.

They would also be suitable for younger pupils who have met the appropriate language and content. They are likely to take about 40 mins but this will depend on the ability of the class to coordinate the different aspects of each task.

The book is aimed at:

Teachers

The idea is to use this as consolidation rather than as a teaching tool. It's worked well with a variety of classes and I've always put the students in pairs to enable them to talk about the methods they're using while they solve the "murder". I've found that their cooperative skills have improved as has their ability to plan and delegate in a bid to "win". I'd suggest a practice run through of one of the "who" suspects the first time you use one of these mysteries to help the class in the organisation process.

Parents

Much more fun than having endless maths exercises to trawl through! Children will engage with the mathematics because it is presented here in an entertaining way. Make sure that your child does know what the key concepts are for each mystery before starting.

Thanks

Thanks must go to the pupils in my classes at Prince Henry's Grammar School who have trialled these activities and suggested names for the suspects. Many will find themselves on these pages.

I hope you and your children enjoy putting on your "detective's hats" and solving these mini murder mysteries.

Jill Whieldon

Mini Murder Mystery 1
Arithmetic

WHO?

Work out these 4 calculations.

Each suspect has made 2 statements.

The murderer has made 2 errors. The victim has made 0 errors.

310 – 213	632 ÷ 8	73 + 26 - 5	29 x 3

Chelsea says
- All the answers are < 100
- 1 answer ends in a "6"

Paris says
- All answers are > 60
- 2 answers end in a "7"

Edward says
- All answers are > 80
- Only 1 answer is even

Mitch says
- The highest answer is the reverse of the lowest answer.
- The 2 closest answers are 4 apart

Jack says
- There are 3 answers in the 90's
- The lowest answer is in the 9 times table.

Lily says
- No answer is under 80
- There are 3 odd answers

WHERE?

Work out each of these pairs of calculations. If the answers are equal choose the 1st letter. If the answers are different choose the 2nd letter. The 7 letters you end up with form an anagram of a British town.

1st calculation	2nd calculation	Choose this if = answers	Choose this if not = answers
26 + 14	65 - 25	C	O
36 x 4	100 - 38	N	W
45 ÷ 9	36 – 20 - 11	I	D
500 – 207	3 x 131	H	R
91 + 19	½ of 200	W	A
57 – 28	3 x 9	C	W
72 ÷ 9	¼ of 32	K	E

WHEN?

Use your "BIDMAS" rules to work out the date and time.

Day:	$3 + 9 \times 2$	Hour:	$52 \div (3 + 1)$
Month:	$36 - 5 \times 7$	Minutes:	$4 + 5 + 6 \times 3$

Year: $1807 + (3 + 2 \times 10^2)$

WHY?

Calculate the following answers for each letter then decode the murderer's statement

a	b	c	d	e
12×5	$20 \div 5$	9×5	$84 \div 7$	$46 - 19$
f	g	h	i	j
$38 - 9$	3×12	$42 \div 6$	6×3	$15 + 26$
k	l	m	n	o
$40 \div 5$	$24 + 29$	9×9	$45 - 6$	$32 - 15$
p	q	r	s	t
7×7	4×8	$35 \div 7$	$27 + 43$	$60 - 16$
u	v	w	x	y or z
$12 + 8$	10×13	$200 - 166$	$72 - 13$	$120 \div 12$

Now decode the murderer's statement

70	7	27	44	7
17	20	36	7	44
70	20	81	81	27
60	39	44	70	17
81	27			

FINAL ACCUSATION

_____ murdered _____

At (place) _____ on (Date) _____ at(time)_____

Why_____

Mini Murder Mystery 2
Money

WHO?

The following suspects each have some of these coins. They can have more than 1 of any. They have added their coins up and stated their total. One of them is impossible. This is the murderer. One of them can be made with no repeated coins. This is the victim.

Jake has 5 coins. The total is 87p	Chloe has 7 coins. The total is £1.32
Phil has 4 coins. The total is 69p	Fiona has 3 coins. The total is £2
Stu has 4 coins. The total is £7	Amy has 6 coins. The total is £1.18

WHERE?

Check every detail of these 4 restaurant bills. 3 contain an error. 1 is completely accurate.
The murder happened at the restaurant where the bill is correct.

Pizza Chef		Burger Hut	
2 margheritas @ £3.99	£7.98	3 double deckers @ £1.87	£5.61
1 pepperoni @ £4.29	£4.29	1 low fat burger @ £1.55	£1.55
2 garlic breads @ £1.56	£2.12	2 colas @ 79p	£1.58
3 lemonades @ £1.35	£4.05	1 milkshake @ 95p	£0.95
Total	£18.44	Total	£9.69

Chicky chuck		Kebab shack	
2 battered wings @ £1.39	£2.78	1 shish kebab @ £2.79	£2.97
2 chip portions @ 89p	£0.89	2 doner kebabs @ £3.25	£6.50
2 side salads @ 97p	£1.94	2 bottles still water @ 58p	£1.16
2 sparkling waters @ £1.09	£2.18	1 coffee @ 75p	£0.75
Total	£7.79	Total	£11.38

WHEN? Find the pair of items that total £10

Mug £3.75	Necklace £6.80	Earrings £4.20	Box chocs £6.35
Handcream £5.02	Glass vase £7.34	Socks £7.25	Flowers £2.66
Dvd £8.34	Scented candle £5.98	Game magazine £4.75	Novel £7.44

If the pair is dvd & flowers it was at 12:30pm
If the pair is mug & socks it was at 5:30pm
If the pair is vase & flowers it was at 7:20am
If the pair is necklace & earrings it was at 11am

WHY? Calculate the answers then decode the message below.

a	b	c	d	e
£10 - £1.60	£3.10 x 3	£10 ÷ 4	£12.80 ÷ 4	£4.50 + £3.50
f	g	h	i	j
£1.75 x 4	£77.70 ÷ 7	£2.06 + £1.04	£6.15 + £4.85	£10 - £3.20
k	l	m	n	o
£10 - £0.40	£18.33 + £1.67	£1.45 + £3.60	£2.95 + 80p	£42 ÷ 8
p	q	r	s	t
48p +90p+£0.62	£20 - £12.50	£6.45 x 3	£1.36 + £3.74	£100 - £85.10
u	v	w	x	y or z
£12.12 x 5	£10 - £4.50	£27.40 ÷ 2	£20 - £10.50	£13.75 x 4

£3.10	£8	£11.10	£8.40	£5.50	£8	£14.90
£3.10	£8	£13.70	£19.35	£5.25	£3.75	£11.10
£2.50	£3.10	£8.40	£3.75	£11.10	£8	£14.90
£5.25	£5.05	£55	£3.20	£8.40	£3.20	!

FINAL ACCUSATION

_____ murdered _____

At (place) _____ on (Date) _____ at(time)_____

Why_____

Mini Murder Mystery 3
Fractions, Decimals and %

**WHO?** One of the 6 characters below has murdered one of the others.
Analyse the number problems to discover the murderer.
Each person has made 3 statements about the calculations.
The murderer has made 3 errors, the victim has made 0 errors.
The others have made 1 or 2 errors.

Statements

A) 40% of 500 is 200
B) Half of 390 is 180
C) 0.6 is the same as 6%
D) 0.25 is the same as 2.5%

E) 0.6 x 300 = 50
F) $\frac{3}{4}$ x 90 = 60
G) Half of $^8/_{10}$ is $^4/_5$
H) 0.085 is the same as $8\frac{1}{2}$%

Katie said
- A is true
- C is true
- D is false

Matthew said
- E is false
- G is false
- B is false

Rebecca said
- C is true
- D is true
- F is true

Daniel said
- D is true
- C is false
- E is true

Leo said
- D is false
- G is false
- H is false

Joanna said
- B is false
- H is true
- G is true

**WHERE?** The murder took place where these are in ascending order:

0.109, $^1/_{10}$, 11% , $^{90}/_{1000}$, 0.099

Nottingham if this order is correct	$^{90}/_{1000}$, 0.099, $^1/_{10}$, 0.109, 11%
Derby if this order is correct	0.109, 0.099, $^1/_{10}$, $^{90}/_{1000}$, 11%
Sheffield if this order is correct	11% , 0.109, $^1/_{10}$, 0.099, $^{90}/_{1000}$
Leicester if this order is correct	$^1/_{10}$, $^{90}/_{1000}$, 11% , 0.099, 0.109

WHEN? Calculate each answer to find the time and date.

Add these fractions together $^5/_8 + 2\,^1/_6$	A) $2\,^6/_{14}$ The time was 6:14pm	B) $2\,^{19}/_{24}$ The time was 19:24
	C) $2\,^6/_{24}$ The time was 6:24pm	D) $^{18}/_{14}$ The time was 8:14pm
Subtract these fractions $2\,^2/_5 - \,^7/_{10}$	A) $1\,^1/_{10}$ The date was 1/1/10	B) $1\,^3/_{10}$ The date was 1/3/10
	C) $1\,^7/_{10}$ The date was 1/7/10	D) $3\,^7/_{10}$ The date was 3/7/10

WHY? Calculate these then decode the message to find the reason for the murder.

a	b	c	d	e
$20 \div 0.5$	$1.8 \times \frac{1}{2}$	$4.5 + 6.5$	$36 \times \frac{3}{4}$	$3 \div \frac{1}{4}$
f	g	h	i	j
$^2/_5 \times 15$	$^3/_{10} \times 5$	$3\frac{7}{8} + 1\frac{1}{8}$	0.95×2	Half of 66
k	l	m	n	o
$^7/_{12} - \,^1/_{12}$	$6 \div \,^1/_5$	$\frac{1}{4} \times 2 \times 2$	0.7×0.7	$\frac{5}{8} \times 4$
p	q	r	s	t
5% of 40	26% as a decimal	15% of 50	$\frac{1}{4} \times \,^4/_5$	10% of 36
u	v	w	x	y or z
$3 \div \frac{3}{4}$	$1.5 \div 2$	$4 - 3\frac{3}{4}$	$^3/_5$ of 30	$1\frac{1}{2} \times 6$

5	12	27	1.9	27	0.49	3.6	30	1.9	0.5	12
6	7.5	40	11	3.6	1.9	2.5	0.49	0.2	40	0.49
27	1.9	30	2.5	0.75	12	3.6	5	12	1	!

FINAL ACCUSATION

_____ murdered _____

At (place) _____ on (Date) _____ at(time)_____

Why_____

Mini Murder Mystery 4
Number types

WHO? One of these 6 people has murdered one of the others. Each has made 3 statements about the following list of numbers. The murderer has made 3 errors. The victim has made 0 errors. The other suspects have made 1 or 2 errors.

5, 6, 13, 16, 21, 38, 49, 52, 61, 64, 72

Harriet says
- There are 5 odd numbers
- There are 2 square numbers
- There are 2 multiples of 7

Joe said
- There are 3 primes
- The difference between the 1st 2 odd numbers in the list is 8
- There are 6 even numbers

Danielle says
- There are 2 multiples of 9 in the list
- The largest gap between numbers is 9.
- The answer to 2^5 is in the list

George says
- The answer to $\sqrt{121}$ is in the list
- There are 2 multiples of 13 in the list
- There are 4 square numbers

Greta says
- 2^4 is in the list
- $\sqrt{169}$ is in the list
- There are no factors of 18 in the list

Zohail says
- 64 is the only cube in the list
- 2^6 is in the list
- There are no multiples of 12

WHERE? The murder was committed in a Midlands town near to Birmingham.

Wolverhampton
Walsall
Dudley
Nuneaton
Birmingham
Kidderminster

It was Wolverhampton if there are 3 prime numbers in the 20's

It was Kidderminster if there are 4 multiples of 30 between 100 and 200

It was Nuneaton if there are exactly 9 factors of 36

It was Walsall if there are 5 perfect square numbers between 50 and 140

Calculate the time and date from these.

The hour part of the time is the answer to	$\sqrt{16} \times (4^2 - \sqrt{121})$
The minute part of the time is the answer to	3^3
The day part of the date is	The 4 factors of 8 added together
The month part of the date is	The 3rd multiple of 4
The year part of the date is	$(10^3 \times \sqrt{4}) + \sqrt{100}$

Calculate these answers then decode the murderer's confession underneath.

a	b	c	d	e
4^2	$\sqrt{100}$	$1^2 + 1^3$	$10^2 \div 4$	$3^2 - \sqrt{4}$
f	g	h	i	j
Next prime after 13	1st prime no in the 20's	$3 + 3^2$	5th prime number	2nd prime × 4th prime
k	l	m	n	o
LCM of 2 & 7	2^2	$\sqrt{169}$	1^{10}	2^3
p	q	r	s	t
HCF of 30 & 45	$5^2 - 1^2$	Cube root of 125	$\sqrt{400}$	$\sqrt{9}$
u	v	w	x	y or z
$\sqrt{36}$	$\sqrt{81}$	$4^2 + 1^2 + 1^2 + 1^2$	9th multiple of 2	$5^2 - \sqrt{9}$

12	7	25	8	7	20	1	3	14	1
8	19	12	8	19	3	8	20	24	6
16	5	7	16	1	6	13	10	7	5

FINAL ACCUSATION

_____ murdered _____

At (place) _____ on (Date) _____ at(time)_____

Why_____

Mini Murder Mystery 5
Negative Numbers

WHO?

The murderer is the person with the highest answer.

The victim is the person with the lowest answer.

-10, -3.5, 0.5, 2.5, -6.5, -7, 1.5, -0.5, -1

Merna worked out the gap from the highest to the lowest

Debbie worked out the highest added to the lowest

Marcus worked out the central number when in order

Adit worked out the total of all the numbers.

Caroline worked out the total of the positive numbers.

Jack worked out the total of the negative numbers

WHERE?

Use the number line to calculate the following answers. The correct one is where the murder happened.

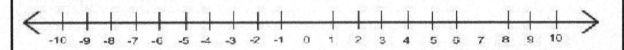

Australia if 7 -12 – 5 + 15 – 4 = -1	South Africa if - 1 – 2 + 8 – 7 = -2
USA if 4 – 3 – 8 + 9 – 2 = - 8	UK if - 5 + 9 – 3 – 7 = - 8

WHEN? The calculation to work out the difference between the 2 temperatures shown is:

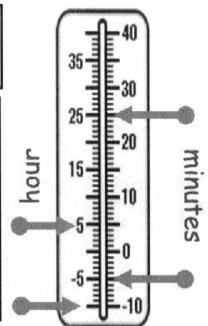

hour   minutes

The correct answer on the left side of the thermometer forms the hours part of the time of the murder

5 - - 10	10 - 5
-10 + 5	5 - 10

The correct answer on the right side of the thermometer forms the minutes part of the time of the murder

25 - 5	5 - 25
25 - - 5	-5 - 25

WHY? Work out the answers then decode the confession of the murderer.

a	b	c	d	e
12-20	-6 + 6	-50 + 20	-9 + 16	100 - 120
f	g	h	i	j
10 - 9	-10 - 8	-10 - 15	3-7	-70 + 10
k	l	m	n	o
1 - 12	40 - 80	-5 + 10	30 - 35	20 - 35
p	q	r	s	t
25 - 37	100 - 150	-6 + 4	-65 + 75	16 - 26
u	v	w	x	y or z
6 - 30	3 - 100	-12 + 24	- 16 + 7	3 - 10

-25	-20	-25	-4	7	5	-7	-30	-8	-40

-30	-24	-40	-8	-10	-15	-2

FINAL ACCUSATION

_____ murdered _____

At (place) _____ on (Date) _____ at(time)_____

Why_____

Mini Murder Mystery 6
Ratio and Proportion

WHO?

6 amounts of £600 have been shared between pairs of friends in different ratios. The victim is the person who received the largest amount of money. The murderer is the person who received exactly half the victim's amount.
Work out all the amounts that the friends received to discover the murderer and victim.

 **Dan** and **Zac** split the money in the ratio 1:2

 **Jasmine** and **Helen** split their £600 in the ratio 2:3

Amy and **Charlotte** split the money in the ratio 5:7

 **George** and **Jake** shared their £600 in the ratio 3:5

 **Matthew** and **Harry** divided their £600 in the ratio 5:1

 **James** and **Ellie** split the money in the ratio 7:3

WHEN?

Cancel all of these ratios to their simplest form.

4 : 6	9 : 12	24 : 2	36 : 24	15 : 40	20 : 100	50 : 30	15 : 18

The date (day:month) is the original ratio that cancelled to 3:4	The time (hrs:mins) is the original ratio that cancelled to 3:8

A recipe for shortbread uses 300g of plain flour, 200g of butter and 100g of caster sugar. The basic recipe makes 12 pieces of shortbread.

In the kitchen cupboard there is 3kg of plain flour, 1 kg of butter and 1.5kg of caster sugar. The maximum number of pieces of shortbread that can be made using the recipe exactly will lead you to the murder spot.

120	The murder took place in the bank
180	The murder took place in the post office
60	The murder took place in the building society
72	The murder took place in the supermarket

In each of these ratios the person receiving the **lower amount** of money gets £12.

Work out the total amount shared out between the pairs each time.

1 : 4	Total = £	Letter A
2 : 3	Total = £	Letter C
7 : 1	Total = £	Letter E
5 : 4	Total = £	Letter G
10: 3	Total = £	Letter H
2 : 1	Total = £	Letter I

1 : 9	Total = £	Letter M
2 : 5	Total = £	Letter O
3 : 7	Total = £	Letter S
6 : 7	Total = £	Letter T
4 : 9	Total = £	Letter U
11: 1	Total = £	Letter W

52	96	27	42	26	26	144	36	30	96
60	40	120	39	30	52	60	40	120	96

FINAL ACCUSATION

_____ murdered _____

At (place) _____ on (Date) _____ at(time)_____

Why_____

Mini Murder Mystery 7
Sequences

WHO?

From the 6 people below you have to decide who the murderer is and who is the victim. Each has made 3 statements about the sequences. The murderer has made 3 errors in their statements. The victim has made no errors. The others have made 1 or 2 errors.

1st sequence	2nd sequence	3rd sequence	4th sequence
1, 5, 9, 13, …	100, 90, 80, 70, …	3, 6, 12, 24, …	80, 40, 20, 10, …

Pete
- The next term in sequence 3 is 48
- The 10th term in sequence 1 is 37
- The rule for sequence 1 is n + 4

Claire
- The 6th term in sequence 4 is 2.5
- The 6th term in sequence 1 is 21
- The rule for sequence 2 is 110-10n

Richard
- The 8th term in sequence 2 is 30
- 192 is the 7th term in sequence 3
- The rule for sequence 1 is 4n + 3

Vicky
- The rule for sequence 3 is 2n
- The 10th term in sequence 2 is 10
- The 6th term in sequence 4 is 2.25

James
- The rule for sequence 3 is 3n
- The 8th term in sequence 1 is 26
- The rule for sequence 4 is n ÷ 2

Chris
- Sequence 4 stays above zero
- The next term in sequence 2 is 60
- -50 is the 15th term in sequence 2

WHERE?

Work out the value of the term indicated in each sequence. Then find the letter of the alphabet that links to your answer. The letters will spell out where the murder took place. For example:
The 4th term of the sequence 3n-10 is 2. The 2nd letter of the alphabet is B .

2nd term of 12n - 4	2nd term of 3n + 2	1st term of 10n - 5
4th term of 2n - 5	3rd term of n²	8th term of 94 – 10n
6th term of 0.5n + 2	4th term of 3n + 1	1st term of 8n - 7

WHEN?

What time comes next in the sequence ?
This is the time of the murder.

What time comes next in the sequence ? This is the time of the murder.

JUNE 2010		JUNE 2010		JUNE 2010
SUN MON TUES WED THURS FRI SAT 1 2 ③ 4 5 6 7 8 9 10 11 12 13 14 15 16 17 18 19 20 21 22 23 24 25 26 27 28 29 30		SUN MON TUES WED THURS FRI SAT 1 2 3 4 5 6 7 8 9 10 11 12 13 ⑭ 15 16 17 18 19 20 21 22 23 24 25 26 27 28 29 30		SUN MON TUES WED THURS FRI SAT 1 2 3 4 5 6 7 8 9 10 11 12 13 14 15 16 17 18 19 20 21 22 23 24 ㉕ 26 27 28 29 30

WHY?

Work out the terms of the sequence $\frac{1}{2}n - 5$

a	b	c	d	e
1st term	25th term	7th term	3rd term	18th term
f	g	h	i	j
24th term	6th term	22nd term	10th term	23rd term
k	l	m	n	o
5th term	13th term	2nd term	16th term	9th term
p	q	r	s	t
11th term	12th term	15th term	19th term	21st term
u	v	w	x	y or z
14th term	4th term	20th term	17th term	8th term

4.5	6	4	7	-0.5	2.5	-2	-0.5	5.5	
-4	-1	7.5	0	2.5	5.5	6	-3.5	-4.5	-1

FINAL ACCUSATION

_____ murdered _____

At (place) _____ on (Date) _____ at(time)_____

Why_____

Mini Murder Mystery 8
Coordinates

WHO? One of the 6 characters below has murdered one of the others. They have each made 3 statements. The murderer has made 3 errors. The victim has made 0 errors. The other suspects have made 1 or 2 errors.

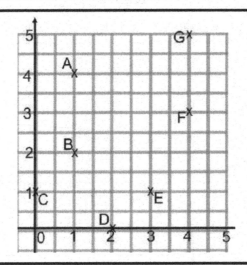

John said
- A is (1,4)
- E is (3,1)
- The x coordinate of G is more than the x coordinate for F

Chris said
- F is (3,4)
- C and E are on the same horizontal line
- The y coordinate of B is less than the y coord of A

Annie said
- G is (5,4)
- C is (1,0)
- B is (2,1)

Sally said
- C and E are on the same vertical line
- A is (4,1)
- D is (2,0)

Russell said
- F is (4,3)
- Joining A to B makes a vertical line
- (4,4) is half way between F and G

Priscilla said
- D is (0,2)
- E is (3,1)
- Joining C,B and G makes a straight diagonal line

WHERE?   The murder was committed within this grid. Following the clues below, you have to mark "x" at the right spot..

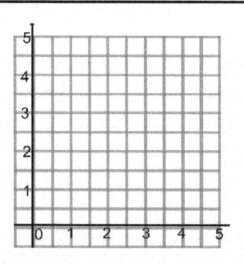

- The x coordinate is 2 more than the y coordinate

- Both of the coordinates are odd numbers

- The total of the coordinates is 4

WHEN?   The time and day of the murder can be decoded from the grid below.

(2,2) (1,1) (1,5) (3,2) (5,2) (5,5)
(3,2) (5,2) (5,3) (4,2) (4,4) (4,1)
(1,2) (3,3)
(5,3) (4,3) (5,2) (1,1) (5,5) (4,2)
(4,5) (1,5) (5,1)

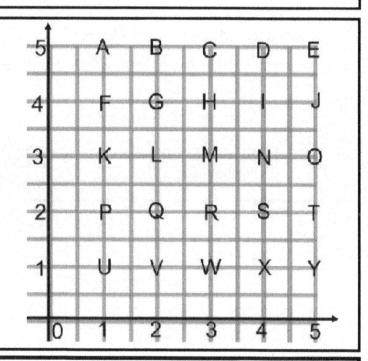

FINAL ACCUSATION

_____ murdered _____

At (place) _____ on (Date) _____ at(time)_____

Mini Murder Mystery 9
Numbers and Mappings

Square numbers	Triangular numbers	Cube numbers	Even numbers
1,4,9,16,...	1,3,6,10,15,...	1,8,27,...	2,4,6,8,...

WHO? The 6 suspects have each made 2 statements about the numbers above.
The murderer has made 2 errors.
The victim has made 0 errors.
The other suspects have made 1 error.
Continue the lists to decide who the murderer and victim are.

Arthur
- The next 2 cube numbers are 64 and 125

- 100 and 120 will both in the square number list.

Leah
- The next 2 triangular numbers are 21 and 28.

- The number 64 will appear in all 4 lists

Tom
- The triangular numbers alternate odd, even, odd, even,...
- 81 will be in the even number list

Emily
- 36 will appear in 3 of the lists

- 55 is only in the triangular number list

Max
- The 25th number in the even number list will be 52

- The 11th number in the triangular number list is 66

Jess
- 100 will be in the square numbers and the even numbers
- The 20th triangular number is 110

WHEN? Work out at what time and on what date the murder happened.

The hours part of the time is the 8th odd number	The minutes part of the time is the 9th triangular number
The month is the 2nd cube number	The date is the 5th square number

WHERE?

The murder took place at the set of coordinates where these 2 mappings cross over each other.

Work out some coordinates for each one, draw each one, then read off where they cross.

$$x \longrightarrow x+2 \quad \text{and} \quad x \longrightarrow 6 - x$$

Mark the position of the murder on the grid

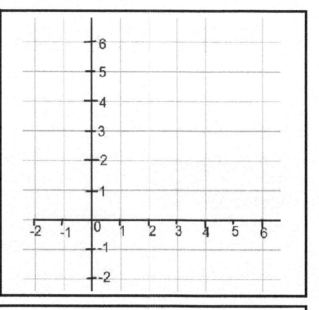

WHY?

Complete the mappings for $x \longrightarrow 10x + 20$
(times by 10, then add 20)

0		Letter s
1		Letter t
2		Letter d
3		Letter w
4		Letter a
5		Letter o
6		Letter f

7		Letter m
8		Letter u
9		Letter r
10		Letter i
11		Letter h
12		Letter e

20	130	140	20	60	120	40	30
50	70	30	120	90	140	20	80
70	100	110	50	60	20	6	!
						6	!

FINAL ACCUSATION

_____ murdered _____

At (place) _____ on (Date) _____ at(time)_____

Why_____

Mini Murder Mystery 10
Expressions & Equations

WHO? Here are 3 facts connecting the ages of 6 different students. The suspects have each written 3 equations. The murderer is the person whose equations are all incorrect. The victim is the person whose equations are all correct.

Claire (C) is 12 years older than Jay (J)	Adam (A) is twice as old as Guy (G)	Lottie (L) is 8 years younger than Uzma (U)

Sian  says	Mike says	Natalie says	Nick says
· C + 12 = J · U + 8 = L · A = 2G	· C + 12 = J · A ÷ 2 = G · L + 8 = U	· L – U = 8 · G = 2A · J – 12 = C	· C – 12 = J · G = $\frac{1}{2}$A · U – 8 = L

WHERE? One of the following expressions simplifies to

$$5a - 3b + c.$$

If it's $3(a - b + c) + 2(a + b - c)$ Then it was in the launderette	If it's $8a + 6b - 2a - c + a - 3b$ Then it was in the post office
If it's $5c - 2b + 2(3a -2c) - (a + b)$ Then it was in the supermarket	If it's $a + 2a + 2a - 2b + b + c$ Then it was in the library
If it's $-4c + 2(3a + b) -5b + 3c$ Then it was in the charity shop	If it's $5(a + c - b) + 4(b - c)$ Then it was in the chemist

WHEN? Match the correct solution of these equations to the date and time of the murder.

$2x - 5 = 12$	If $x = 3.5$ it was half past 3am	If $x = 8.5$ it was half past 8am
	If $x = 17$ it was 5pm	If $x = 7$ it was 7 am
$10 - 4x = 8$	If $x = 0.5$ it was in 2005	If $x = 2$ it was in 2002
	If $x = -0.5$ it was in 1995	If $x = -2$ it was in 1998
$2(5x+1) = 18$	If $x = 3$ it was on 3rd	If $x = 2$ it was on the 2nd
	If $x = 0.6$ it was on 6th	If $x = 1.6$ it was on the 16th
$x - 1 = 3x - 5$	If $x = 2$ it was February	If $x = 1$ it was January
	If $x = 3$ it was March	If $x = 4$ it was April

WHY? Solve each equation first.

a	b	c	d	e
$x + 1 = 6$	$2x - 1 = 11$	$29 - x = 2$	$13x - 10 = 16$	$2(x + 1) = 3$
f	g	h	i	j
$2x + 3 = 17$	$10 - 2x = 8$	$3x - 7 = 20$	$3(2x + 1) = 63$	$3x - 7 = 2$
k	l	m	n	o
$x - 4 = 12$	$x + 1 = 15$	$4x - 5 = 39$	$2x - 7 = 2$	$4x + 1 = 11$
p	q	r	s	t
$2x - 8 = 16$	$2x - 9 = 31$	$5x - 12 = 28$	$x + 3 = 20$	$8x - 8 = -8$
u	v	w	x	y or z
$2x + 5 = 35$	$10x = 180$	$2x + 6 = 9$	$2x + 9 = 16$	$10x + 1 = 3$

9	0.5	0	9	2.5	15	1	9	0	3.5

12	14	15	17	0.2	1.5	5	17	5	4.5

0.5	20	15	5	0	10	2.5	4.5

FINAL ACCUSATION

_____ murdered _____

At (place) _____ on (Date) _____ at(time)_____

Why_____

Mini Murder Mystery 11
Perimeter & Area

 **WHO?**

Here are 8 rectangles. They are not drawn accurately.
The 6 suspects have each made 2 statements about the area or perimeter of the rectangles. The victim has made 0 errors and the murderer has made 2 errors. The other 4 suspects have each made 1

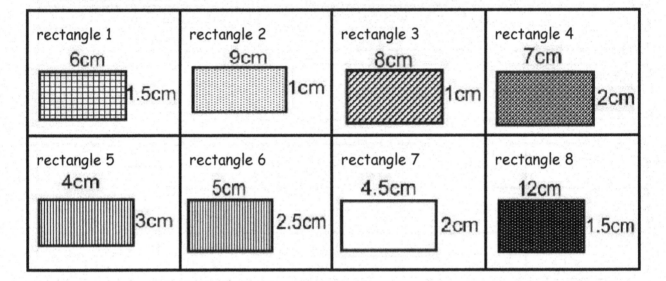

rectangle 1
6cm
1.5cm

rectangle 2
9cm
1cm

rectangle 3
8cm
1cm

rectangle 4
7cm
2cm

rectangle 5
4cm
3cm

rectangle 6
5cm
2.5cm

rectangle 7
4.5cm
2cm

rectangle 8
12cm
1.5cm

Sean said
- The perimeters of rectangles 1 and 6 are the same.
- Rectangle 8 has the largest area.

Tilly said
- The areas of rectangles 2 and 4 are the same.
- Rectangle 3 has the smallest area.

Kira said
- The perimeter of rectangle 6 is 15cm
- The area of rectangle 5 is 14cm²

Ross said
- The area of rectangle 8 is 12.5cm²
- The area of rectangle 1 is 9cm²

Toby said
- The perimeter of rectangle 3 is 18cm
- The area of rectangle 6 is 10.5cm2

Helena said
- The shortest perimeter is rectangle 6
- The longest perimeter is 26cm

WHERE?

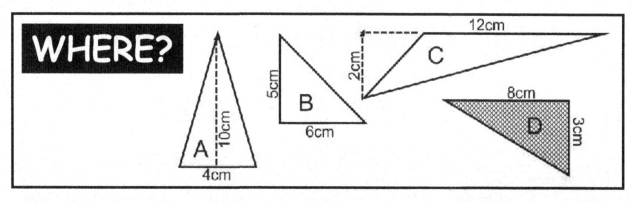

It happened at the butchers if...	Triangle A has the largest area
It happened at the bakers if..	Triangle B's area is 30cm²
It happened at the chemist if...	Triangle C has a larger area than triangle D
It happened at the greengrocers if...	Triangle B has the smallest area.

WHEN?

| The month part of the date is the length of a square whose area is 49cm² | The day part of the date is the perimeter of the same square. |
| The hours part of the time is the area of a 9 by 2 rectangle. | The minutes part of the time is the perimeter of the same rectangle. |

WHY?

On each individual shape, the edges are equal lengths. Calculate the length of one side on each shape then put them in ascending order.

| P = 30 cm | P = 50 cm | P = 28cm | P = 48cm | P = 60cm |

He thought area was measured in cm.	✚ ⬡ ⬠ ▢ ☆
He said 1m² = 100cm²	▢ ⬠ ⬡ ☆ ✚
He said 1m = 1000 cm	✚ ⬡ ☆ ▢ ⬠
He measured perimeter in cm²	⬡ ☆ ▢ ⬠ ✚

FINAL ACCUSATION

_____ murdered _____

At (place) _____ on (Date) _____ at(time)_____

Why_____

Mini Murder Mystery 12
Lines & Angles

None of the diagrams is accurately drawn. You need to calculate, not measure.

WHO?

Each of the 6 suspects has made 2 statements about the lines and angles in this diagram. The murderer has made 2 errors. The victim has made 0 errors. The others have made 1.

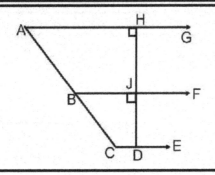

Homer says
• Line BF and AG are parallel
• Angle BCD is obtuse

Marge says
• Line HD is perpendicular to AG
• Line CD and JB will intersect

Maggie says
• There are 2 right angles in the diagram
• Angle JBA is obtuse

Lisa says
• Lines BC and JD are parallel
• Angle BCD is a reflex angle

Bartholemew says
• There are 8 right angles in the diagram
• Line AC will never intersect line HD

Ned says
• Angle HAB is acute
• Angle JBC is obtuse

WHEN?

The size of the missing angle in these shapes tells you the time and date of the murder

Hours part of time
Triangle. 130, 30, ...

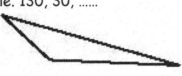

Minutes part of time
Quadrilateral. 140,100, 75, ...

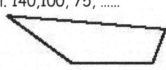

Date.
Straight line split into 6 equal parts ......

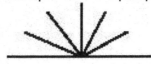

Month.
Right angle. 56, 23, ...

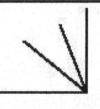

WHERE?

Work out the lettered angles then decode the place where the murder happened.

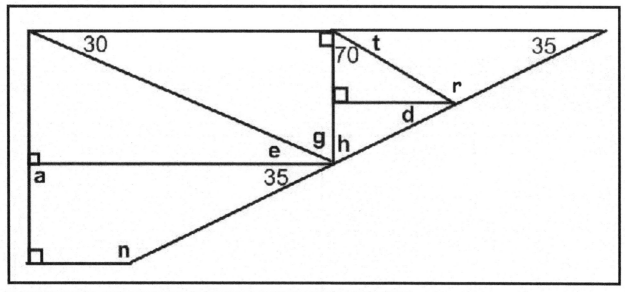

90	20	20	55	30	60	90	125

35	30	145	60	90	20	30	

WHAT?

The implement was one of the following shapes. Use the description to work out which it was.

Square	Trapezium	Rhombus	Isosceles triangle	Equilateral triangle	Regular pentagon

The implement has at least 2 equal sides	The implement has a pair of parallel sides
The implement has at least 1 right angle	The implement has no line of symmetry
The implement has 1 obtuse angle	The implement has 1 acute angle

FINAL ACCUSATION

_____ murdered _____

At (place) _____ on (Date) _____ at(time)_____

With a _____

Mini Murder Mystery 13
3-D

WHO?

Each suspect has made 3 statements about the solids shown here. The murderer has made 3 errors. The victim has made 0 errors. The others have made 1 or 2 errors.

Cube	Octahedron	Cuboid	Tetrahedron
Square based pyramid	Triangular prism	Pentagonal prism	Dodecahedron

Peter said
- The cube has 8 vertices
- The tetrahedron has 6 edges
- The pentagonal prism has 7 faces

Libby said
- The dodecahedron has 12 faces
- The triangular prism has 6 vertices
- The cuboid has 8 edges

Rhys said
- The square based pyramid has 4 faces
- The dodecahedron has 60 edges
- The Tetrahedron has 4 vertices

Vicky said
- The pentagonal prism has 10 edges
- The triangular prism has 5 faces
- The cuboid has 8 vertices

Laura said
- The octahedron has 8 edges
- The dodecahedron has 12 vertices
- The triangular prism has 6 faces

Ellie said
- The octahedron has 8 faces
- The triangular prism has 9 edges
- The square based pyramid has 4 vertices

WHERE?

This cuboid's volume is 60cm³. The murder happened at the place connected to the correct set of measurements.

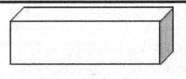

The maths classroom if the measurements are	12cm by 2cm by 3cm
The English classroom if the measurements are	1.5cm by 6cm by 8cm
The history classroom if the measurements are	10cm by 12cm by 0.5cm
The geography classroom if the measurements are	30cm by 2 cm by 2 cm

WHEN?

The hours part of the time is the volume of a cuboid measuring 6cm by 2 cm by 1.5 cm.	The minutes part of the time is the area of the largest face on the same cuboid
The date is the length of an edge of a cube whose volume is 64cm³.	The month is the volume of a cube whose length is 2cm.

IMPLEMENT?

The object had a curved surface	There was no vertex on the object
There was at least 1 flat surface	The curved surface unfolds to make a rectangle
Was it a ...	

Hemisphere	Cone	Sphere	Cylinder

WHY?

One of these volume calculations is correct for this triangular prism.
The reason is connected to the correct calculation.

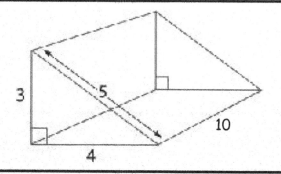

3 x 4 x 5 x 10	He thought that a rectangle was a 3d shape
0.5 x 3 x 4 x 10	He confused a prism with a pyramid
$(5 \times 10) + \frac{1}{2}(3 \times 4)$	He said a hemisphere was half a circle
$(3 + 4 + 5) \times 10$	He said if you halve a cube you get a smaller cube

FINAL ACCUSATION

_____ murdered _____

At (place) _____ on (Date) _____ at(time)_____

With (implement)_____

Mini Murder Mystery 14
Mean, Median, Mode, Range

WHO?

One of these 6 people has murdered one of the others. The suspects have all calculated the mean, median, mode and range of the set of data shown in the diagram. The murderer has made 4 errors, the victim has made 0 errors. The others have 1,2 or 3 errors.

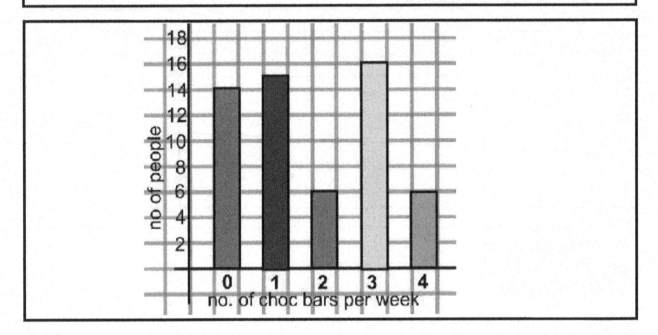

no. of choc bars per week

no of people

Alyson said the following
- Mode = 3
- Median = 1
- Mean = 75.42
- Range = 5

Rob said the following
- Mode = 3
- Median = 2
- Mean = 11.4
- Range = 4

Georgina said the following
- Mode = 16
- Median = 2
- Mean = 1.98
- Range = 5

Dawn said the following
- Mode = 2 and 4
- Median = 1
- Mean = 1.98
- Range = 4

Chris said the following
- Mode = 3
- Median = 1
- Mean = 1.74
- Range = 4

Richard said the following
- Mode = 6
- Median = 2
- Mean = 1.74
- Range = 4

WHEN? Work out the date and time when the murder took place by analysing the following data.
You must find a day, and month then a time.
All will be numerical like 23/11 would be 23rd Nov and 16:35 would be 25 to 5 pm

The day is the mean of this set of data	23, 32, 15, 39,31
The month is the median of the data	1.2, 1.9, 2.8, 2.9, 2.1, 2.1, 0.9, 2.7, 1.8, 1.0
The hour part of the time is the missing number x that would make the mean of these 4 numbers 20.	28, 29, 9, x
The minutes part of the time is the range of	23, 32, 15, 39,31

WHERE? The murder took place in a Yorkshire town. By analysing the data decide in which of the 4 towns it happened.

This stem and leaf diagram shows the ages of the 13 people who were close to the place the murder was committed.

```
1 | 0 4 4 4 6
2 | 1 3 5
3 | 6 7 7 9 9
```

It was committed in York if the mode is 14, the median is 23 and the range is 8
It was committed in Harrogate if the mode is 4, the median is 23 and the range is 29
It was committed in Leeds if the mode is 14 and the median is 23 and the range is 9
It was committed in Doncaster if the mode is 14, the median is 23 and the range is 29

WHY? One of these sets of 7 numbers has a mode, median, mean and range all = 5. This will link to the reason for the murder.

3,4,5,5,5,6,7	Because he said medium instead of median
3,3,5,5,5,6,8	Because he forgot to write the numbers in order for the median
8,5,5,5,4,3,3	Because he forgot to divide for the mean
5,5,5,5,5,5,5	Because he left the range as a calculation, not a single answer

FINAL ACCUSATION

_____ murdered _____

At (place) _____ on (Date) _____ at(time)_____

Why_____

Mini Murder Mystery 15
Data Display

WHO? A murder has taken place at a department store.
There are 6 suspects.
These diagrams each show the number of employees aged between 20 and 30.

Here is some extra information about other age groups at the same store.
• There are 12 people between 30 – (40).
• The angle on the pie chart for the 40 – (50) year age group is 60°
• The symbol on the pictogram for the 50 – (60) year age group is

You need to complete each chart first then analyse the 6 sets of statements below.

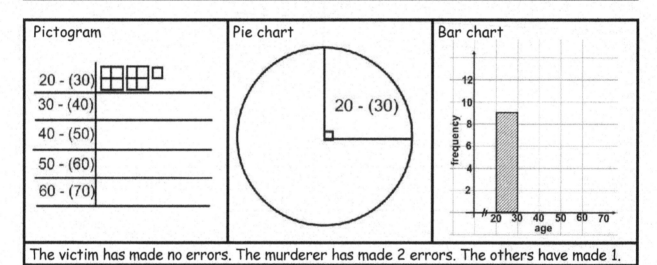

Pictogram

20 - (30)	
30 - (40)	
40 - (50)	
50 - (60)	
60 - (70)	

Pie chart

20 - (30)

Bar chart

The victim has made no errors. The murderer has made 2 errors. The others have made 1.

Imogen said
• The modal age group is 30 – (40)
• The angle for the the 30 – (40) group is 180°

Zac said
• The 40-(50) group symbol is
• The angles for the 2 groups aged 50 and more add up to 90°

Matthew said
• There are twice as many people in their 30's as in their 40's
• The oldest age group has the highest bar

Gabi said
• ¼ of the employees are in their 20's
• There are 40 people altogether

Maddy said
• The smallest angle is 30°
• The 60-(70) symbol is

James said
• There are 36 people altogether
• There are 6 people in their 50's

WHERE?

These are the prices of 24 items. Tally this data to find out where the murder happened.

£2.40	£3.86	£2.80	£7.25	£2.49	£4.99	£2.50	£5.00
£2.55	£1.90	£4.50	£1.75	£4.78	£8.90	£6.00	£2.50
£3.50	£2.99	£7.50	£2.50	£9.75	£7.00	£2.00	£3.80

price (p)	tally
$0 \le p < £2.50$	
$£2.50 \le p < £5$	
$£5 \le p < £7.50$	
$£7.50 \le p < £10$	

kitchen department
if the tally for
£2.50-£5 is

gents department
if the tally for
£7.50-£10 is ||||

furniture department
if the tally for
£5-£7.50 is ||||| |

perfume department
if the tally for
£0 - £2.50 is ||||| |

WHEN?

This pie chart shows the angles for the sales of different types of ladieswear.

It was at lunchtime if there were 180 tops sold	It was just before opening time if 25 trousers were sold
It was at morning coffee break if 40 dresses were sold	It was at closing time if 35 skirts were sold

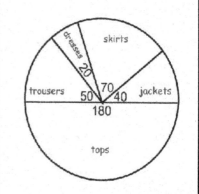

In total 720 items were sold

WHY?

This % bar chart shows how long the employees have worked at the department store.

0%   50%   100%

Legend:
0-2 years
2 - 4 years
4 - 6 years
over 6 years

Because he ate my sandwich	If 50% have worked there for 2-4 years
Because he took my parking space	If 90% have worked there for 4-6 years
Because he wants my job	If 10% have worked there for over 6 years
Because he got a promotion before me	If 60% have worked there for 2-4 years

FINAL ACCUSATION

_____ murdered _____

At (place) _____ on (Date) _____ at(time)_____

Why_____

Mini Murder Mystery 16
Probability

WHO?

The 2 way table shows the number of right and left handed girls and boys in a class. Beneath are some statements from 4 suspects. The murderer has made a mistake in one of their statements. The 3 innocent people have not made a mistake. Identify the murderer.

	boys	girls
Right handed	15	10
Left handed	2	3

Ambreen
- There are 30 people in the class.
- The probability of selecting a left handed child at random from the class is $1/6$.

Sophie
- The probability of selecting a right hander from the class is $5/6$.
- The probability that a girl is left handed is $3/10$.

Ellie
- There are 25 right handers.
- The probability of selecting a boy from the left handed pupils is $2/5$.

Beth
- The probability of selecting a girl from the right handed pupils is $2/5$.
- There are 4 more boys than girls.

WHERE?

From the histogram decide which statement leads to the place where the murder happened.

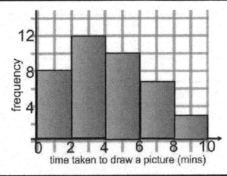

time taken to draw a picture (mins)

It was in the hall if......   The probability of someone taking 2-4 mins is 12 %
It was in the lounge if......   The probability of someone taking over 4 mins is 50%
It was in the dining room if......   There are 9 people who took 4-6 mins
It was in the kitchen if......   The probability of someone taking 6-10 mins is 10%

WHEN? You need to work out the time of day and the date from the following clues.
The time will be given in the form "15:46" and the date as " 14/05 for the 14th May"

The hour part of the time is the probability of selecting a **T** from the word **MATHS**. Write your answer as a percentage

The minutes part of the time is the probability of selecting a **D** from the word **MURDERED**. Write your answer as a percentage

The day part of the date is the probability of selecting an **L** from the word **CALCULATED**. Write your answer as a percentage

The month part of the date is the probability of selecting a **T** from the word **CALCULATED**. Write your answer as a percentage

WHY? Change each of these fractions into a percentage (rounded to the nearest whole number).

a	b	c	d	e
$1/4$	$5/9$	$5/8$	$7/10$	$1/100$
f	g	h	i	j
$1/50$	$2/5$	$7/12$	$1/20$	$3/4$
k	l	m	n	o
$1/5$	$2/15$	$1/2$	$19/20$	$3/50$
p	q	r	s	t
$1/25$	$17/50$	$8/11$	$9/20$	$3/40$
u	v	w	x	y or z
$10/19$	$2/7$	$3/10$	$17/20$	$1/3$

Now decode the statement

56	1	63	25	53	45	1	58	1	4
73	6	56	25	56	13	33	13	5	20
1	45	56	5	45	63	53	5	8	45

FINAL ACCUSATION

_____ committed the murder

At (place) _____ on (Date) _____ at(time)_____

Why_____

Answers

Task	Murderer	Victim	place	date	time	reason
1	Jack	Paris	Warwick	21/1/2010	13:27	She thought sum meant some
2	Phil	Jake	Burger Hut		7:20am	He gave the wrong change to my dad !
3	Rebecca	Matthew	Nottingham	1/7/10	19:24	He didn't like fractions and I love them !
4	Danielle	Joe	Nuneaton	15/12/2010	20:27	He doesn't know how to square a number
5	Merna	Jack	South Africa		15:30	He hid my calculator
6	Amy	Matthew	Building Society	9th Dec	15:40	He gat twice as much as me
7	James	Claire	The cinema	6th July 2010	7:55	She forgot my birthday
8	Annie	Russell	(3,1)	Tuesday	$\frac{1}{4}$ to 6 pm	
9	Tom	Emily	(2,4)	25th Aug	15:45	She said two times four was 6 !
10	Natalie	Nick	supermarket	Feb 16th 2005	8:30am	He thought x plus y was an equation
11	Helena	Sean	butchers	28th July	18:22	He said 1m = 1000cm
12	Lisa	Homer	At the garden gate	30th Nov	20:45	Implement...With a trapezium
13	Laura	Peter	history (with cylinder)	4th Aug	18:12	He confused a prism with a pyramid.
14	Georgina	Chris	Doncaster	28th Feb	14:24	He didn't put numbers in order for the median
15	Maddy	Zac	Gents department	Morning	coffee time	Because he wants my job
16	Sophie		lounge	20th Oct	20:25	Because he probably likes biscuits